MACALESTER

The Booksmith Group
A DIVISION OF RP

Published in the United States of America by

an imprint of

A wholly owned subsidiary of Southwestern/Great American, Inc.
P. O. Box 305142
Nashville, TN 37230
1-800-358-0560
www.thebooksmithgroup.com

ISBN (Standard): 978-1-934892-06-0
ISBN (Premium): 978-1-934892-19-0

Library of Congress Control Number: 2008930685

Publisher: Stephen D. Giddens
Managing Editor: Jennifer Dawn Day
Associate Editor: Heidi L. T. Tuey
Photo Editor: Bobby Sagmiller, VisibilityCreative.com
Text: Erin Peterson
Book Design: Kirsten Howard
Photography: Stephen Gardner, PixelWorksStudio.net,
Additional Photos from Macalester College Archives

Printed in the United States of America
First printing 2008

TABLE OF CONTENTS

the Character *of* Macalester

It is no accident that one enduring symbol of Macalester College is the multicolored woven tartan. The Macalester experience itself is a fabric woven of multiple values: academic excellence informed and enriched by diverse cultural and international perspectives and a commitment to service and civic engagement.

Macalester's character can be traced back to its Scottish Presbyterian roots. Founder Edward Duffield Neill set out to provide a first-rate education for people who lived on the nation's frontier. Like other Presbyterian colleges, Macalester was open to students and faculty of other faiths, and the college encouraged students to use their educations to step forward and be of service in the world.

Today, frontiers are not limited to geography. Macalester's inclusiveness now encompasses far greater religious, cultural, economic, and international diversity than Neill could have imagined. The scope of activities of Macalester faculty, students, and alumni—and their reach throughout the world—might astonish those who helped establish and nurture Macalester College.

And yet the man whose life's work included presidential cabinet member, battlefield chaplain, frontier churchman, and pioneer educator would surely recognize in Macalester and its alumni much of himself and of the college he envisioned. And he would be proud.

TARTAN

Mac folks have always been proud of the Scottish roots of the college's namesake, Charles Macalester. Students and faculty members attending early Founders Day celebrations, for example, were encouraged to wear plenty of plaid, and the onetime "Tartan Troupers" were volunteer entertainers who performed at nursing homes, prisons, and community centers.

Since 1948, when Clan MacAlister adopted the college, the clan's official tartan—a bright red plaid—has been worn by generations of Macites.

An echo of this tartan can be found on Macalester's official logo, the stylized tartan shield. The logo celebrates Macalester's origins, and at the same time its style suggests the streets of a city, the crossroads of the world, and an openness to the future.

HIGHLIGHTS

1885   Originally a preparatory school, Macalester begins offering college-level classes.

1889   The first class, 10 men, graduates in the spring. Six go on to do religious work, two become lawyers, one becomes a physician, and one becomes a teacher.

1893   The college admits its first three women in the fall.

1900   An early mission program of the Presbyterian Church sends Macalester students around the world.

1915   Catharine Deaver Lealtad becomes Macalester's first African American graduate. (See Lealtad's biography, page 139.)

1919   President Elmer Bess creates a social service major that addresses subjects including child welfare and immigration.

1927   Tuition increases nearly 17 percent—from $150 to $175 a year.

1942   With the help of President Charles Turck, Esther Torii is released from a Japanese American detention camp in Portland, Oregon, specifically to attend Macalester. (See her biography, page 140.)

1943   The Macalester Intercultural Forum discussion group forms to "encourage discussion of problems relating to the divergent cultural groups that make up the people of the United States."

1946   Yahya Armajani, a Middle East historian from Tehran, Iran, is hired by President Turck. (See Armajani's biography, page 141.)

1946   In response to U.S. needs following World War II, the college adds courses in vocational areas including nursing, education, and business.

1946–47 Programs including the Student Project for Amity Among Nations (SPAN) and the Mexican Caravan are developed to give students international experiences.

From L to R: *Young Esther Torii on campus, Main and Main West Halls, early Mac students, Kofi Annan gets off to a quick start, graduates process from Kirk Hall, Hubert Humphrey with students*

1950   *1962*

1950   Believing that the United Nations is the world's best hope for lasting peace, President Turck raises the flag of the five-year-old organization. It still flies today.

1950   Sociology professor Paul M. Berry assigns his race relations class an investigation of race relations in the Twin Cities.

1950   Poet Robert Frost speaks at a convocation.

1950s   The Cosmopolitan Club, a group of international and U.S. students, starts to organize International Weekends that draw college students from throughout the region

1960   Richard Nixon, vice president of the United States, speaks at Macalester. His appearance, arranged by the Republican Club, helps boost the group's membership to more than 250 students. Nixon receives a lifetime membership in the club.

1961   Kofi Annan graduates from Macalester. The future U.N. Secretary-General and Nobel Laureate is state champion orator, a member of the track team, and president of the Cosmopolitan Club as a student.

1961   Macalester opens its International Center, providing a central location for study abroad information. The same year, the college establishes the World Press Institute, designed to increase international understanding of the United States by offering journalists from around the world an intensive introduction to the country and its people.

1961   Macalester commits to a more ambitious admissions program, which includes attracting at least 20 percent of its students from outside the Midwest as well as students from a range of financial and social backgrounds.

1961   Macalester drops its Bachelor of Science degrees as well as degrees in journalism and medical technology, returning to a more traditional liberal arts curriculum. Dean Lucius Garvin encourages Macalester to develop two "steeples of strength": the sciences and international programs.

1962   An exchange program is established with two predominantly black colleges, Morehouse College in Atlanta and Knoxville College in Tennessee.

1967   1968   1969

1962   Poet and humorist Ogden Nash gives a talk on campus.

1967   The first of 36 international students from Europe, Asia, Latin America, and the Middle East participate in
Macalester's International Leader Scholars and Wallace International Scholars programs. The programs are
designed to identify and support people with leadership potential in their home countries.

1968   The Hubert H. Humphrey Professorship in International Affairs is endowed to bring international scholars of the
highest caliber to teach at Macalester.

1969   The new Expanded Educational Opportunities program brings 75 first-year students of color to Macalester.

1969   President Arthur S. Flemming creates a more flexible curriculum and abolishes certain graduation requirements
including freshman English, physical education, religion, foreign language, and speech. He also encourages
interdepartmental programs, a precursor to modern interdisciplinary study programs.
(The faculty later establishes new graduation requirements and updates them periodically.)

1969   The first Indian Week is celebrated with a powwow, bilingual chapel service, speakers on Indian education
and welfare, and a Buffy Sainte-Marie concert.

*From L to R: President Arthur Flemming, soon-to-be Justice Antonin Scalia and ACLU President Norman Dorsen, studious students,
Dean Ahmed Samatar at International Roundtable*

1988

1994

1972   Macalester celebrates its first Hispanic Week with the theme "Awareness, Education and Unity."

1979   The college hosts a 10-day Vietnam symposium to discuss policy-making and activism during and after the war. Speakers including former Kennedy aide Arthur Schlesinger, antiwar activist Daniel Berrigan, and national and local journalists.

1980   Russian poet Joseph Brodsky speaks at Macalester.

1981   George McGovern, former U.S. Senator and 1972 presidential candidate, speaks on "The Cold War Reconsidered."

1986   As part of a DeWitt Wallace Conference on the Liberal Arts, former chief justice Warren Burger, soon-to-be justice Antonin Scalia, ACLU president Norman Dorsen, and author John Edgar Wideman join with others to speak on the 200th anniversary of the U.S. Constitution.

1987   A special conference explores the emerging policy of openness in the Soviet Union.

1988   Macalester establishes a Community Service Office to foster an ethic of lifelong service in all members of the Macalester community.

1992   Macalester's new strategic plan reinforces the college's emphasis on academic excellence, internationalism, diversity, and community service. The plan's goals are to attract students and faculty from a greater diversity of nations as well as ethnic and economic backgrounds, increase the size of the faculty, strengthen academic programs including the International Studies program, make study-abroad opportunities available to more students and faculty, and have students volunteer their time in the community in meaningful ways.

1993   Former U.S. president Jimmy Carter and former vice president Walter Mondale '50 speak at the college.

1994   Ahmed Samatar is appointed to the newly created position of Dean of International Studies and Programming. He initiates Macalester's International Roundtable, which annually brings world scholars to campus to discuss global issues such as ethnicity and identity, the environment, and the role of literature, arts, and culture in an era of globalization.

1995   The first Faculty Development International Seminar, also organized by Dean Samatar, engages a group of Macalester faculty in seminars and research with overseas colleagues. Destinations for the seminars have included Hungary, Brazil, South Africa, Malaysia, Turkey, Taiwan, the People's Republic of China, Israel, and Palestine.

2002   Joi Lewis becomes Macalester's first Dean of Multicultural Life. To help Macalester be more inclusive in its work, her office organizes programming for students, faculty, and staff.

2003   Macalester becomes a founding member of Project Pericles, an organization that encourages colleges and universities to include social responsibility and participatory citizenship in their educational programs.

2004   Macalester students contribute more than 50,000 hours to the community, working with education programs, human service organizations, environmental and arts organizations, and more. Over the course of their college careers, 92 percent of Macalester students volunteer in the community.

2005   President Brian Rosenberg announces the creation of an Institute for Global Citizenship, which integrates programs and services that help prepare students for lives as global citizen leaders, encourage innovative scholarship, and promote new models of service which increase the level of benefit to both the community and the student. The Community Service Office, now part of the IGC, changes its name to Civic Engagement Center.

From L to R: *Volunteers with Habitat for Humanity, a recycling center, an agency serving African-born Minnesotans, Hurricane Katrina cleanup*

2006

2005   Professor Jane Rhodes becomes Macalester's first Dean for the Study of Race and Ethnicity, whose goal is to engage the campus community in exploring the roles of race and ethnicity in the history and structure of U.S. society.

2006   In January, 21 students and seven staff members from Macalester travel to Gulfport, Mississippi, to assist with relief efforts for victims of Hurricane Katrina.

"Right on Lake Street" exhibition

2006   Nobel Prize-winning author Toni Morrison speaks at opening convocation.

2007   In collaboration with the University of Maastricht in the Netherlands, Macalester begins a new study abroad program focusing on Globalization in Comparative Perspective.

2007   Two Mideast peace advocates, Palestinian Hanan Ashrawi and Israeli Yossi Beilin, discuss possible solutions to conflicts that divide the Middle East, as part of a speaker series on peace and conflict. Former Ambassador Richard Holbrooke and former Vice President Walter Mondale '50 also participate in the series.

2007   "Right on Lake Street," a public history exhibit based on research by students in 12 different Macalester courses, opens at the Minnesota History Center. The user-friendly exhibit focuses on Minneapolis's Lake Street as a dynamic and changing focal point for long-settled ethnic groups and more recent immigrant communities.

2008   The Peace Corps announces that Macalester ranks 16th among small colleges in the number of alumni serving in the Peace Corps, with 17 current volunteers. Since the Peace Corps was established in 1961, 307 Macalester alumni have volunteered around the world.

2008   Macalester awards honorary degrees to philanthropist Shelby M. C. Davis, founder of the Davis United World College Scholars Program, and Philip Geier, the program's executive director. The Davis program annually supports study at U.S. colleges for hundreds of students from around the world. In May, 33 students from 28 countries make up the first class of Davis Scholars to graduate from Macalester.

Toni Morrison speaks, Shelby M. C. Davis meets with students.

A SENSE OF PLACE

Geography is a discipline founded on the idea that place matters. Not only does it affect what we do, it shapes who we are.

Perhaps no one understood this better than geographer Hildegard Binder Johnson. She fled Nazi Germany in 1934 and spent years searching for a place to call home before she met President Charles Turck in 1947. She convinced him that she was the ideal candidate to start a brand-new geography department at Macalester. Her sterling academic credentials and published research made his decision easy.

Johnson had great enthusiasm for the discipline, wide-ranging curiosity, and a commitment to both scholarly and community activities. She encouraged geographic education at all levels, and she championed the idea of conservation long before it was a popular cause.

Two decades into her career at Macalester, times had changed. Urban riots dominated the news in the late 1960s, and the college sought to increase its commitment to social engagement. Johnson was eager to add an urban geographer to provide a new perspective on this cultural shift.

David Lanegran '63 proved to be the perfect fit. He had studied under Johnson while at Macalester, and he wanted to use his skills to create change in the inner city. He joined the faculty in 1969.

Lanegran soon launched a field research seminar—and later a series of studies—focused on Grand Avenue. He and his students explored how neighborhood associations and businesses could encourage economic growth and create safe, livable spaces. Their research provided the groundwork for many of the changes that have helped make Grand Avenue the vibrant and successful place it is today.

Lanegran led similar projects in other areas of the Twin Cities. He and his students provided basic research for neighborhood organizations that couldn't afford to hire planning firms. Lanegran's teaching, and the urban studies concentration he introduced, inspired generations of students to take action as urban planners and citizens in their own neighborhoods.

Among them was Laura Smith '94, who had taken classes and done summer research with Lanegran. Five years after she graduated, she joined the department as a professor.

Smith began her career at another important juncture for the discipline. Technological advances, such as geographic information systems (GIS), were changing the way that geographers collected and analyzed data. Through her courses, Smith and her students have used GIS in field research on topics such as transportation, economic development, and housing foreclosures. The issues have changed over the years, but students continue to contribute useful research on important issues to community groups, and many go on to careers ranging from historic preservation to meteorology.

Today, the Geography Department is one of the largest on campus, and Johnson's influence remains. At the beginning of a methods course required for all majors, Smith invites Lanegran to give a short lecture about the pioneering woman who introduced geography to the college and her enduring commitment to the discipline and the community.

Hildegard Binder Johnson's sterling academic credentials and published research made President Turck's decision easy.

Hildegard Binder Johnson

Lanegran's teaching and the urban studies concentration he introduced inspired generations of students to take action as urban planners and citizens in their own neighborhoods.

David Lanegran '63

Laura Smith '94

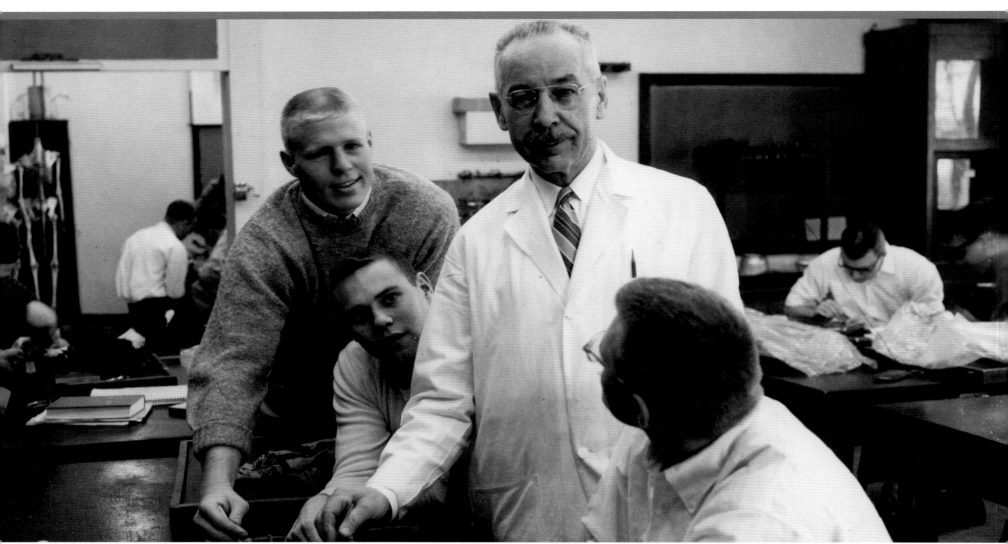

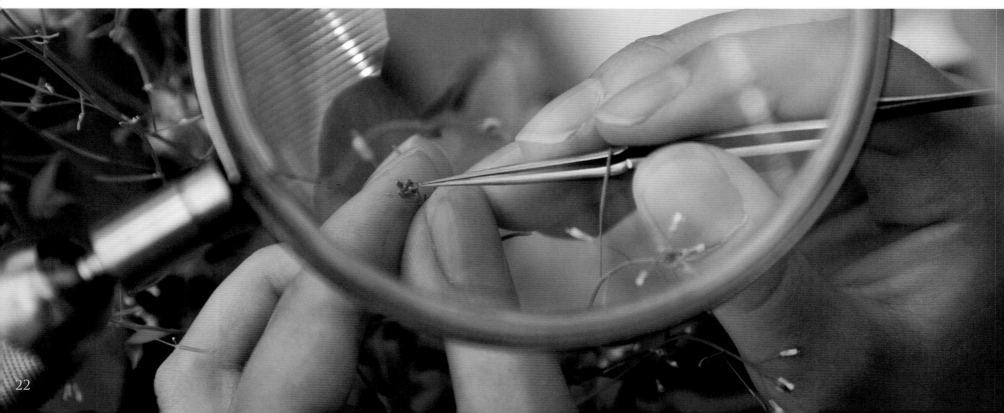

THE SCIENCE OF SUCCESS

O. T. Walter wasn't a doctor, but medicine got a boost when he joined Macalester as a biology professor in 1922. A gentle, thoughtful professor who demanded excellence from his students, he helped hundreds of Macites take their first steps toward health-care careers. Former students who went on to become doctors remember him as a mentor who inspired their passion for biology and the world around them. Many continue to be grateful for his willingness to write recommendation letters that helped them get into top medical schools.

A deeply religious man, Walter believed his calling was to bring out the best in his students and encourage them to look beyond themselves. He once wrote that he felt a "responsibility to help each student realize the fullness of his personality and his inherent talents . . . [and] to prepare him for leadership with integrity rather than expediency, so that he may identify himself with causes greater than himself in the service of mankind." For his 41 years in the classroom, he remained devoted to this goal.

After his death, Walter's former students funded a professorship to recognize and honor his contributions to the college. In 1999, Jan Serie, a widely respected transplant immunologist who had been at the college since 1983, was named to the endowed O. T. Walter Professorship. Her teaching style is not unlike Walter's: former students have described her as both demanding and engaging, and as someone who helps students raise their own expectations.

Serie has been more than just a fine teacher; she played an integral role in the metamorphosis of the department. When she started at the college in 1983, she was one of just three female professors in the science division and one of very few young women professors at the college. (She politely declined an invitation to join the faculty wives club early in her career.) She has served as a role model for younger women professors, and today there are almost equal numbers of men and women faculty members. She also helped transform the department offerings to a hands-on, research-based curriculum. Serie also directed the college's Center for Scholarship and Teaching, which is dedicated to helping professors become better and more innovative teachers.

Professor O. T. Walter encouraged students to look beyond themselves.

In addition to the Walter Professorship, Walter's legacy lives on through the O. T. and Kathryn Walter Prize. The honor, which includes a cash prize, is given to up to four seniors who choose work related to medicine. Can Sungur '07, a recent recipient of the award, attributes his decision to pursue cancer research at the University of Minnesota to the encouragement of Mac professors.

Professor Jan Serie has played an integral role in developing research-based instruction in the sciences at Macalester.

Political science professor Ted Mitau was one of Macalester's most engaging professors.

GREAT EXPECTATIONS

Macalester's Political Science Department has a reputation for launching countless alumni into successful careers, from top political leaders to heads of nonprofit organizations. Professors have long required the highest caliber work in the classroom while also pushing students to put their political ideas into practice in their communities.

Professor Theodore G. Mitau '40 helped set the tone for the department when he began teaching in the 1940s. He didn't allow students to sit back and listen to lectures—he called on everyone in his wide-ranging discussions, often inviting students to his home to continue conversations. He helped organize students who wanted to help in political campaigns—one notable example came in 1948, when he recruited student volunteers to help out with Hubert Humphrey's sucessful campaign for the U.S. Senate. Among them was a promising young student named Walter Mondale. In his lectures, he demanded that students see the nuances and subtlety of real-world situations, and one of his favorite sayings was "The world is not black or white. It is gray!" His students recognized that when he expected more of them, they could deliver. As a result, they began to ask more of themselves.

In 1968, after 28 years of teaching at Macalester, he became chancellor of the Minnesota State College system. He is remembered today through the G. Theodore Mitau Endowed Professorship in Political Science, which was established by Timothy Hultquist '72. When Chuck Green arrived on campus in 1965, he took some cues from Mitau, who had hired him. He demanded the best from his students, and he took that expectation for performance one step further. He wanted his students to leave the classroom and go into the community, using all the tools they had developed in their studies to make a positive impact.

In Green's organizational courses, he taught students about administrative behavior. But rather than testing what students learned only through exams and papers, he had them link up with schools, nonprofit organizations, and political campaigns that needed help solving organizational problems. Students were expected to be more than interns; they were expected to be peers.

Political science professor Chuck Green

Political science professor Ted Mitau

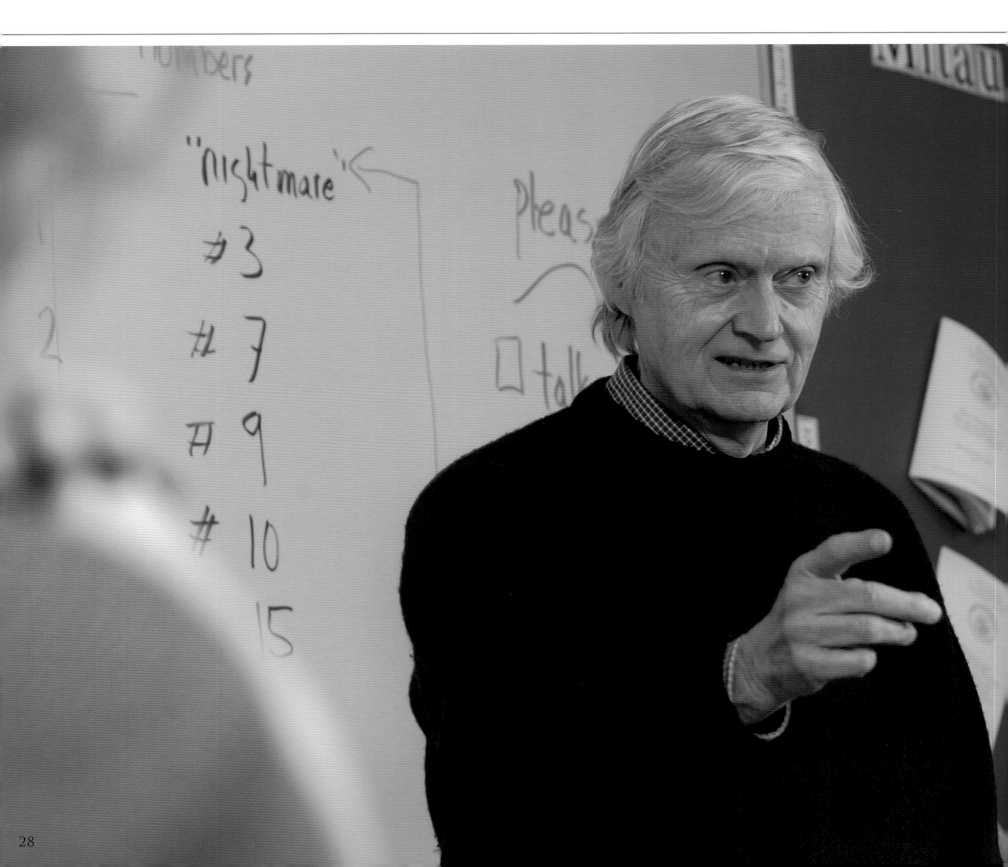

Green wanted students to see that these real problems had real consequences, and that broad theories must be adapted to fit individual organizations. Students did planning, surveys, and consulting, and they offered solutions as the organizations moved forward. Students learned that their books provided a starting point, but they also had to use their own ingenuity to solve difficult organizational issues.

This type of work is an essential, not optional, part of a liberal arts education, Green believes. Students have a responsibility to make contributions to democratic life, and at a college in a richly diverse metropolitan area, they can get started right away.

The philosophy he taught his students—that they had not only the capacity to take action but the responsibility to do so—often led them to pursue volunteer activities and careers in nonprofits and outreach organizations. Many acknowledge that they took paths in life that they would not have considered without him.

Even after Green's retirement in 2005, his philosophies live on through the Chuck Green Civic Engagement Fellowship, offered to as many as a dozen students each year. After a solid academic grounding in a topic during spring semester, "Green Fellows" spend a summer working with clients of their choosing on specific problems. A different professor each year heads up the course, and Paul Dosh, who led the 2007 course, says that he pushes students to create something that lasts beyond themselves. Students have helped groups increase their legislative clout, raise money for their projects, and create advocacy publications.

Professors in the Political Science Department have changed over the years, but the lesson they impart to students has changed little: great work can begin in the classroom, but it rarely ends there.

GREAT WORK CAN BEGIN IN THE CLASSROOM, BUT IT RARELY ENDS THERE.

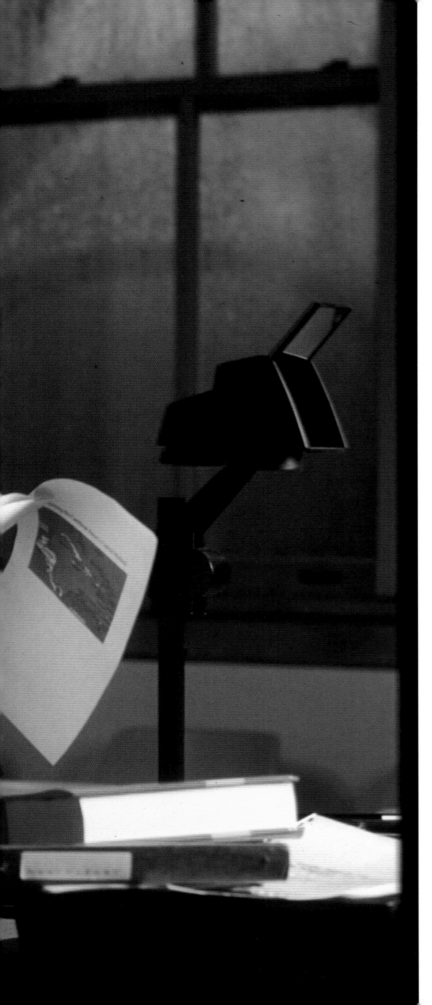

BEYOND NUMBERS

Mac students who graduate with a degree in economics may be savvy with numbers and finances, but they'll also be the first to tell you that the best investments aren't made in the stock market. They're made in relationships.

Graduates go on to serve in top positions at prestigious firms, including Morgan Stanley, JPMorgan, and Goldman Sachs. Others apply their expertise in the nonprofit sector at organizations including the Brookings Institution and the Center for Energy, Economic, and Environmental Policy. They rarely forget their roots.

They return to the college as guest lecturers, talk with students about career paths, participate in fundraising and other committees, and serve on the college's Board of Trustees.

Many economics graduates trace their success to Professor Karl Egge, who always saw his role not just to teach students the principles of economics, but to help students secure good, meaningful jobs after graduation. He taught skills for success in the business world, and he's even been known to give lessons on appropriate business etiquette, right down to lessons on firm handshakes.

Egge, who arrived on campus in 1970 and began phased retirement in 2006, has cultivated strong relationships with students, alumni, and top financial firms and other organizations. He frequently arranges lunches between students and speakers, sends packages of senior résumés to alumni who might be hiring, and happily provides recommendations to employers looking to hire Macalester graduates.

THE BEST INVESTMENTS AREN'T MADE IN THE STOCK MARKET. THEY'RE MADE IN RELATIONSHIPS.

Egge has long touted the range of options students have, from banking and consulting to technology, teaching, and nonprofit work. And with about half of recent economics alumni hailing from outside the United States, many of them pursue jobs internationally, further broadening the reach of Macalester graduates and future opportunities for students.

Although Egge is no longer teaching full-time, his legacy will live on through the Egge Visiting Professorship. Hundreds of former students contributed to the fund, which will be used to hire someone who has spent time outside of the classroom—most likely on Wall Street—to teach classes and to continue to build the Macalester economics network.

Thanks to Egge and many others in the Economics Department, students become adept at more than just financial analysis: They learn the importance of developing friendships and long-lasting connections. They know it's always a good decision to put stock in bonds.

Professor Karl Egge

MANY ECONOMICS GRADUATES TRACE
THEIR SUCCESS TO PROFESSOR KARL EGGE.

GETTING TO KNOW ALL ABOUT YOU

you

When David McCurdy arrived at Macalester in 1966, he was charged with a formidable task: to create an Anthropology Department from scratch. McCurdy jokes that there were misgivings on both sides. He was apprehensive about the weather, which was seven below zero on the January day he interviewed for the position. Macalester administrators, who had hoped to hire a mid-career anthropologist, may have been reluctant to hire McCurdy, who was fresh out of graduate school.

Nonetheless, the Anthropology Department was an immediate hit, with more than 100 students taking introductory classes alone. Before long, McCurdy got permission to hire friend and fellow anthropologist James Spradley.

The two worked together frequently on research and publications, but perhaps their best known work is *The Cultural Experience*, a book on ethnographic interviewing that has taught generations of undergraduate students how to do research to understand the customs of people and cultures. The work, published in 1972, caused a stir in the field.

While significant anthropological research required months, if not years, in the field, McCurdy and Spradley's interviewing technique helped its users tease out a great deal of information in just a few interviews. Their book made it possible for undergraduate students to conduct field research during a single semester. Through their research, students got a close look at many microcultures: firefighters, third-grade students, and hitchhikers, among others.

Some of McCurdy's colleagues from other institutions believed that undergraduates should study theory, not conduct their own research. But McCurdy insisted the opposite was true: anthropology taught people to see the world through the eyes of others, and students gained a far greater understanding of the discipline by conducting their own research.

Significant student research was just one of the groundbreaking aspects of the work. The best student work was published in *The Cultural Experience*, a résumé-boosting accomplishment for any undergraduate. The two editions of *The Cultural Experience* showcase dozens of ethnographies done by students. Their subjects have included groups such as Jehovah's Witnesses and members of a car theft ring, and all of them have broken new ground in the small worlds studied.

Though most students do not pursue graduate study in anthropology, many say the techniques they've learned have benefited them in their careers as, for example, teachers, doctors, and managers. One alumnus, now a sports editor at a daily newspaper, says the interview techniques he learned from the class still help him in his job today.

Spradley passed away in 1982 and McCurdy retired in 2004, but their technique continues to be taught today. Professor Dianna Shandy, who joined the department in 1999, was a co-author for the 2004 edition of the book that included new student ethnographies. She says she became a proponent of the technique as an undergraduate.

From Top, *Professors Spradley, Shandy, McCurdy*

McCurdy and Shandy say their goal is to create better anthropologists and better citizens. As people around the world become increasingly interconnected, the ability to see a situation from multiple viewpoints grows more important. And developing that skill begins by understanding the perspectives of those who live just down the block.

WORLDLY MATTERS

When anthropologist Jack Weatherford traveled to Mongolia a decade ago, he quite literally wanted to follow in the footsteps of Genghis Khan. He spent years traveling the path of the 13th-century emperor to learn more about him, and eventually turned his journey into a *New York Times* bestseller. *Genghis Khan and the Making of the Modern World* (Crown, 2004) is an absorbing work about Khan's life and legacy. In the process of researching and writing the book, Weatherford built a link between Macalester and Mongolia that's been a boon to both the college and the country.

During the research process, he brought students with him to help with fieldwork, and he frequently shared material he gathered from his travels during his classes. Some students became so inspired by the work they did with Weatherford that they carried it even further. One former student, Lauren Bonilla, went to work for a company devoted to Mongolian travel. Two groups of students have helped create bilingual books to help Mongolian children learn English.

The cultural exchange isn't limited to Macalester students. Thanks in part to connections built by Weatherford, mathematics and computer science professor Michael Schneider earned a Fulbright grant to do work with a Mongolian university, and several Mongolian students have enrolled at Macalester. Alumni even have traveled to Mongolia through the college. In the right hands, places that are half a world away seem very close to home.

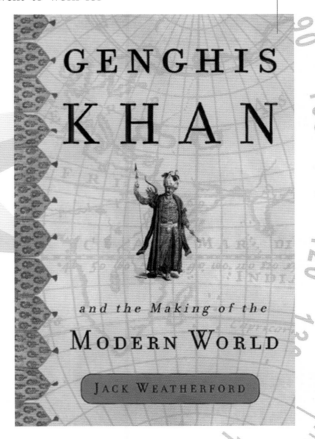

GENGHIS KHAN and the Making of the MODERN WORLD

JACK WEATHERFORD

NOBEL PURSUITS

Kofi Annan, then-Secretary-General of the United Nations, paused during a day on campus with Macalester President Brian C. Rosenberg, Dr. Carol Rosenberg, and their sons, Adam (left) and Sam.

Kofi Annan may be Macalester's best-known Nobel Prize winner, but he's not the only person with Macalester connections linked to the prestigious Swedish prize.

Kofi Annan '61

Nobel Connection:

Annan was awarded the Nobel Peace Prize in 2001. He shared the award with the United Nations.

Worthy Work:

During his tenure as Secretary-General of the United Nations, Annan worked to bring peace and emphasized the organization's responsibilities with regard to human rights. With his help, the United Nations addressed global challenges including HIV/AIDS and international terrorism.

Notable Quote:

"Today's real borders are not between nations, but between powerful and powerless, free and fettered, privileged and humiliated. Today, no walls can separate humanitarian or human rights crises in one part of the world from national security crises in another." (From the Nobel Lecture, December 10, 2001)

Macalester Fact:

When he first arrived at Macalester, Annan refused to wear earmuffs, which he found unattractive. A cold winter's day quickly cured him of his bias and taught him a lesson that served him well in many of his endeavors: "Never walk into an environment and assume that you understand it better than the people who live there."

NOBEL PURSUITS

Jeff Halper '68

Nobel Connection:

Halper was nominated for a Nobel Peace Prize in 2006.

Worthy Work:

Halper is the coordinator of a coalition of human rights groups called the Israeli Committee Against House Demolitions. His work has sought to find a peaceful solution that recognizes the rights of both Palestinians and Israelis and ends the Israeli occupation of the West Bank and Gaza.

Notable Quote:

"We think, as Israelis, that Jews and Arabs should live together," Halper says. "Palestinians have rights of self-determination just like we have. We have to fight also for their rights. One of our slogans is 'we refuse to be their enemies.'" (From "Profiles of Peace," American Friends Service Committee)

Macalester Fact:

As a student at Macalester, Halper was involved in both civil rights and antiwar activities.

He received a Distinguished Citizen Citation from Macalester in 2003.

Mary Montgomery, biology professor

Nobel Connection:

While still a graduate student, Montgomery was the third author on a paper that earned the 2006 Nobel Prize in Physiology or Medicine. She attended the ceremony in December 2006.

Worthy Work:

The work of Montgomery and her colleagues explained the mechanism behind a process that turns off particular genes in an organism, known as RNAi. Knowledge of this process may open up new avenues of research on diseases including AIDS and cancer.

Notable Quote:

"Follow the science. It's good to have a planned set of experiments to explore a particular phenomenon, but one should be flexible enough to change course based on the results of previous experiments."

Macalester Fact:

When Montgomery arrived at Macalester in 1998, it was just after a major storm had passed through, ripping the roof off the home she'd rented. She spent two nights sleeping in her office before she arranged to rent a college-owned apartment. "And yet," she muses, "I was thrilled to be here and starting my dream job."

the Campus *of* Macalester

Tucked neatly into a few square blocks in St. Paul, Minnesota, Macalester's campus holds distinctive memories. Crackling cold weather, for one—especially memorable for students from warm climates who make their first snow angels or toss their first snowballs as Mac students. The comfortable feeling of a residential neighborhood.

The daily path from dorm to classroom, and from one class to the next—at first a struggle to find, and eventually so familiar our feet could carry us even if our brains were trained on something else. The places we shared with everyone, and those favorite spots—a lab or a corner of the library or a quiet place outdoors—that we thought of as our own.

Most importantly, Macalester's campus is where we met faculty, staff, and fellow students who changed our lives. Behind the actual doors of Macalester's buildings, other doors were opened—to new ideas, new possibilities, new selves—and we never looked back.

At left: *First-year students prepare for Freshman Camp (photograph undated)*

Pushball, which appeared on campus decades ago, has been revived, and the Pipe Band has marched on for more than 50 years.

BUILT TO LAST

1884

In 1885, Macalester's campus was one multipurpose building at the edge of a cornfield. Over time, it has grown to include seven academic buildings, a library, a campus center, a chapel, an athletic and recreation center, 10 residence halls, five language houses, a handful of theme residences, and several buildings that house student services and administrative offices.

1884   Main Hall is built. The college's first major building, intended as the east wing, stood for more than 100 years before being razed to make room for the new library.

1887   Main Hall West is completed. "Old Main" has been on the National Historic Register since 1977. Once home to the entire college, it now houses most departments in the humanities division.

1907   Wallace Hall, originally a women's dormitory, is dedicated to and named for James Wallace as he concludes his presidency and returns to the faculty. Described by one newspaper as "absolutely fireproof," it has proved its longevity. In 2003, the building was renovated and the attic was finished to provide housing for sophomores.

1910   The Carnegie Science Hall is completed through a gift from Andrew Carnegie. The structure is built at a cost of $50,000. It currently houses social science departments.

1923   A campus gym and field house is built for $200,000, billed by *The Mac Weekly* as "finest in [the] Northwest." Before its construction, basketball players traveled a mile each day to get to practice.

From L to R: *Kirk Hall, Carnegie Hall, Weyerhaeuser Library, pre-stadium playing field, Bell Tower, Stadium*

1927   1942   1952

1927 Kirk Hall opens, named in honor of trustee Robert Kirk's son, Everett.

1927 A president's residence is constructed at 1644 Summit Avenue, a gift from department store founder George Draper Dayton. In the 1980s it becomes the Hugh S. Alexander Alumni House.

1928 The Bell Tower, which houses one of the first bells ever delivered to Minnesota, is funded and built by the classes of 1927 and 1928.

1942 Weyerhaeuser Library (now Weyerhaeuser Hall) is dedicated. Originally a library holding more than 100,000 volumes, it is now home to administrative offices.

1947 Bigelow Hall is built. The dormitory—along with temporary living structures built along St. Clair Avenue known as "Macville"—helps accommodate the huge influx of students returning to college at the end of WWII.

1952 Winton Health Center opens. The building is named in honor of the parents of trustee David Winton. (In fall 2008, its services moved to the college's new athletic and wellness complex, the Leonard Center.)

1961   1970   1988   1997

1961   The International Center opens at 1635 Summit Avenue, providing services to students planning to study abroad as well as international students and the World Press Institute. Alex Haley writes a first draft of the 1976 novel *Roots* while staying at the center. In 1999, the center moved to its current location at 1576 Summit Avenue.

1964   Dupre Hall and Doty Hall open. Dupre is named after J. Huntley Dupre, history professor and academic dean of the college from 1951 to 1961. Doty is named after Margaret Doty, dean of women from 1924 to 1960.

1965   The Janet Wallace Fine Arts Center is dedicated. DeWitt Wallace, who provides funding for the building, names the center after his mother, the wife of James Wallace.

1965   The Olin Hall of Science is dedicated, funded through a donation from the Olin Corporation.

1969   Weyerhaeuser Memorial Chapel is dedicated. The unique hexagonal structure features bronze-tinted glass and seats 375.

1970   The Rice Hall of Science is dedicated. Like its Olin counterpart, the building is funded by the Olin Foundation, but it is named for former Macalester president Harvey Rice.

1974   Kagin Commons, a dining facility built in the 1960s, is named for history professor Edwin Kagin.

1988   The DeWitt Wallace Library opens. The building is designed to accommodate a third of the student body at any one time and features computer terminals, Internet access, and built-in flexibility for future technological developments.

1997   An extensive renovation of the Olin-Rice Science Center is completed, dramatically expanding space for teaching labs and for interdepartmental collaboration. The center houses a Foucault pendulum, a 225-pound, 30-foot instrument that extends from the third floor to the main lobby.

1998   George Draper Dayton residence hall opens; it features suites suitable for juniors and seniors.

2001   The Ruth Stricker Dayton Campus Center opens. Named for an alumna, trustee, and major donor, the campus hub houses Café Mac, space for meetings and student organizations, a campus store, and other services. Also, a major renovation to Kagin Commons makes it a center for student services including career advising, internship and community service placements, and a multicultural life center, along with a ballroom used for large campus events.

2003

2007

2008

2003   Macalester flips the switch on one of the first urban wind turbines in the nation. The Class of 2003 helps fund the tower's installation.

2007   Construction begins on the Leonard Center, which features a gym, field house, natatorium, fitness center, health services offices, locker rooms, and an office suite for the Athletics Department. More than 90 percent of the materials from the previous field house, gym, and natatorium are reused or recycled. The facility opens its doors in 2008.

2008   Ground is broken for the new home of Macalester's Institute for Global Citizenship (IGC). The building is designed to qualify for LEED platinum certification, the highest level of environmentally friendly design. The Leonard Center is dedicated. In addition, preliminary planning is underway for renovation and expansion of the Janet Wallace Fine Arts Center.

From L to R: *Janet Wallace Fine Arts Center, Weyerhaeuser Memorial Chapel, Olin-Rice Science Center, George Draper Dayton residence hall, rendering of Institute for Global Citizenship building*

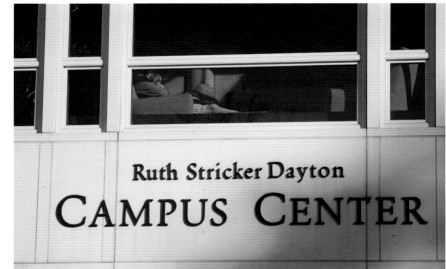

2003:
MACALESTER FLIPS
THE SWITCH ON
ONE OF THE FIRST
URBAN WIND TURBINES
IN THE NATION.

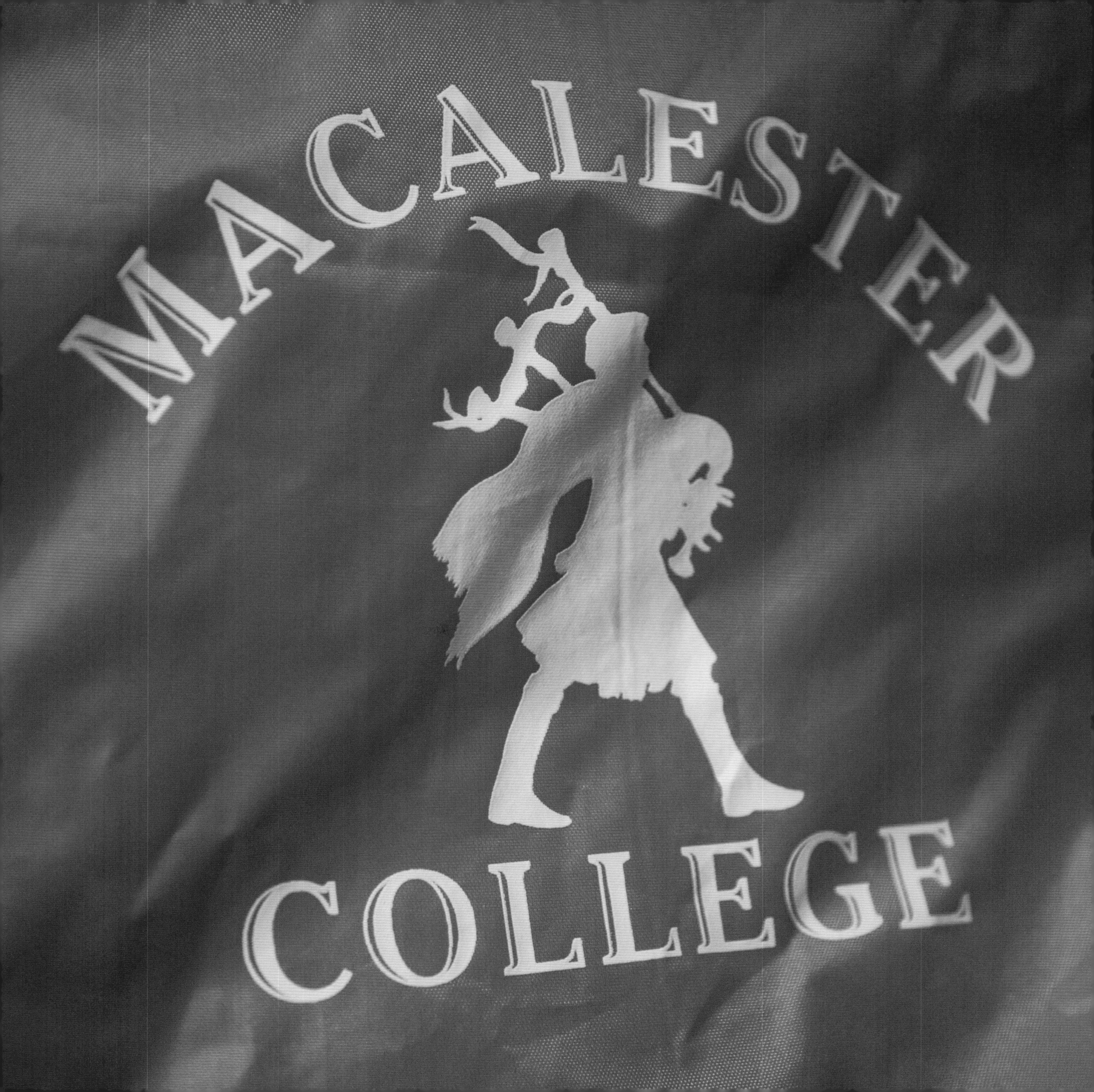
MACALESTER
COLLEGE

CIRCA 1910:
MACALESTER'S CAMPUS INCLUDES MAIN HALL
AND ADJACENT MAIN HALL WEST (CENTER),
CARNEGIE SCIENCE HALL (LEFT OF MAIN HALL WEST),
AND WALLACE HALL (TOP CENTER).

ROCK TO REMEMBER

The song says diamonds are a girl's best friend, but for Mac students, the rock closest to their hearts is a 700-pound behemoth that sits just outside of Old Main and the Library.

A "gift" from the class of 1908—the students rolled it from the corner of Cambridge and Grand to a spot near the center of campus—it's been through its share of hijinks. During its first 100 years, it was rolled out to the corner of Snelling and Grand and later stolen by a group of Carleton students (who returned it by mail, cash on delivery). It's been spray painted by people hoping to create art—and by people just hoping to advertise the party happening Friday night. When the college created a new Macalester logo in the 1990s, at least one person joked that perhaps the rock would be sculpted into a tartan shield. Though it hasn't gotten much rest, the next hundred years promise just as many adventures.

THE BELL

The bell that sits in the tower near Weyerhaeuser Hall is more than just a way to summon the Macalester community to convocations and other college events: it's a vital part of the college's history. The bell was obtained from college founder Edward Duffield Neill and was manufactured in 1855, making it one of the oldest bells in St. Paul. The classes of 1927 and 1928 provided funding for the Bell Tower.

Like the rock, it's been the object of the occasional practical joke. In 1978, the bell was removed from the tower on Christmas Eve and mysteriously appeared at House of Hope Presbyterian church about a mile from campus. The caper made headlines in the local papers when the church's pastor (and one-time Macalester trustee), Reverend Calvin Didier, said it would be returned to the college only when "the faculty and students return[ed] to the church and renew[ed] the time-honored affiliation we once had." Some saw sharpness in the challenge; others say the remark was meant in good humor. The bell returned to the college shortly thereafter and has remained on campus ever since.

IF THESE WALLS COULD TALK

Most Mac alumni will tell you that some of their most valuable lessons came from life on campus—especially from dorm life, where they learned to share their rooms and their lives with others

Late nights with friends, music on the radio, and plenty of clever pranks are hallmarks of every generation of dorm dwellers at Macalester. Perhaps everyone has taken a break from the books at some point to instigate, participate in, or at least watch a snowball fight.

Alumni also vividly recall the cheap (if nutritionally dubious) food they bought in bulk and kept in their rooms to stave off hunger between meals. For some it was Spam, for others it was popcorn, and for still others it was ramen. Those with jobs in the dining hall who brought back extra desserts often received a hero's welcome.

Many have memories more specific to their eras swatting bats with tennis rackets in Wally Hall, listening to Bruce Springsteen blasting endlessly on dorm-room radios, and ordering endless pizzas for delivery from Green Mill

Residence Halls—as well as off-campus houses—have always been more than just a place to study and sleep: Just like classrooms, dorms are the starting point for wide-ranging discussions. At Macalester, the fiercely debated topics are likely to include war or poverty or existentialism. But they are equally likely to be about whether a game was properly called "Duck, Duck, Goose" or "Duck, Duck, Gray Duck," or whether couscous is best served with chicken or lamb.

Dorms are a place to learn to understand and accept differences among people, and a place where people learn to compromise and negotiate. Most importantly, they are the starting point for lifelong friendships.

RELIGIOUS TRADITIONS

The scope of religious life at Macalester today is dramatically broader than founder Edward Duffield Neill could have imagined. Nonetheless, he would certainly find links between the two eras. Many of Macalester's enduring values have their roots in the Presbyterian faith: a commitment to service, openness to new knowledge, and an active interest in the world as a whole.

Neill, a Presbyterian minister, worked hard to establish a connection between the college and the Presbyterian Synod. In 1880, the church gave Macalester $30,000 to endow the presidency, and the school officially became a college of the synod. The connection benefited both the synod and Macalester: the school got a steady stream of students from the church, and the college served as a base for educating future Presbyterian ministers. In the Presbyterian tradition, Macalester had always been open to other faiths, hiring a rabbi to teach Hebrew just a few years after the college's founding. "We're proud that we're tied to a church that's very open and progressive in many ways, one of which is multi-faith engagement," says college chaplain Lucy Forster-Smith.

The college maintained prominent Presbyterian ties through required chapel services, religious studies courses, and other means. By the late 1960s, students who came to Macalester were more varied in their beliefs, and requirements of all sorts were being eliminated. However, while many colleges dropped their church affiliations, Macalester maintained—and continues to maintain—a covenant with the church.

Forster-Smith sees a great resurgence of interest in religious and spiritual groups today. Ten very active student groups represent a variety of faiths. In addition, programs created through Lilly Endowment grants that Macalester received in 2001 and 2006 have enabled dozens of students to explore religion and vocation seriously through a series of activities including internships with religious and nonprofit organizations.

THE MAC EXPERIENCE

When they're not hitting the books, Mac students can often be found participating on one of the dozens of extracurriculars on campus. Some organizations such as *The Mac Weekly*, which was founded in 1914, are long-standing institutions; others form as student interests develop.

By 2008, more than 100 organizations ranged from cultural groups to Amnesty International, Women in Science and Math, and Minnesota Nice.

Preparing to plant native seeds for a "green roof" at Macalester, creating a commissioned mural in a St. Paul neighborhood

"WORKING ON THE MAC WEEKLY DEFINED MY COLLEGE LIFE," SAYS KATE HAVELIN '83. "I KNEW I'D BE A WRITER, AND I STILL KEEP UP WITH SOME OF THE WEEKLY CREW."

Below, demonstrating that it is possible to ride a square-wheeled bicycle

"I REMEMBER
MARCHING
IN A WINTER
CARNIVAL PARADE
WITH THE
BAGPIPE BAND
AT 8 DEGREES
BELOW ZERO."

— BARBARA JAMES SCHUE '57

The arts bring people together, entertain us, and nearly always invite us to see things in new ways. That's why they have always been an important part of campus life. For some, participation in the arts meant countless hours rehearsing and preparing for performances, creating visual art, or tapping away at a keyboard for the literary journal. Others participated as viewers, listeners, audience members.

There's no question that Macalester alumni have made their mark in the arts world. Tim O'Brien '68 received the National Book Award in 1979 for *Going After Cacciato*. Steve Coleman '92 earned a Tony Award for *Russell Simmons Def Poetry Jam*, a work he co-wrote and in which he co-starred. Producer Roy Gabay '85 has a Tony for *A View from the Bridge*, named Best Play of 1998. The Sounds of Blackness, founded by Macite Russell Knighton '72 and led since 1971 by Gary Hines '74, has collected three Grammy Awards. Percussionist Joey Waronker '93 has worked with musicians including R.E.M., Beck, Paul McCartney, Johnny Cash, and Nelly Furtado. Other Mac arts luminaries include sculptors Duane Hanson '46 and Siah Armajani '63, Civil Rights photographer Flip Schulke '54, playwrights Jessica Blank '97 and Danai Gurira '01, Hüsker Dü musician Bob Mould '82, author Charles Baxter '69, film producer Lynn Niederfeld Morgan '68, and actor-producer Peter Berg '84. Still other alumni have become friends and patrons of the arts; a prominent example is potter and arts advocate Joan Adams Mondale '52, who during her years of public life was known as "Joan of Arts."

And whether the work led to a career in the field or a handful of memories relived at reunions, they are an integral part of the Macalester community, bringing people together to read, listen, watch, and be entertained.

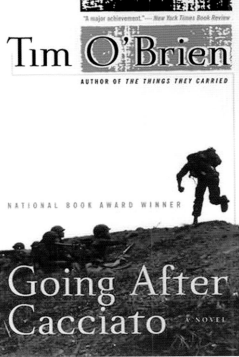

Inscription. *David Chioni Moore, professor of English and chair of international studies and longtime scholar of writer Langston Hughes, purchased a signed copy of a 1960 paperback by the noted Harlem Renaissance author. Inside, in Hughes's large, cursive handwriting, was an inscription to a longtime Macalester political science professor:*

> *"Inscribed*
> *To Dorothy Dodge*
> *with the regard of*
> *Langston Hughes*
> *Lagos, Nigeria*
> *July 5, 1962."*

Faculty members clockwise, from upper left: *Dorothy Dodge, political science; David Chioni Moore, English and international studies; Mary Gwen Owen, speech and theater; Virginia Schubert, French; Jerry Webers, geology; Andy Overman, classics*

WINNING TRADITIONS
(AND LOSING)

The first Macalester students had barely cracked the spines on their books when they began creating a sporting tradition at the school. Members of the first Macalester class took a break from their studies on the very first day to play a game of baseball. After forming an official team the following spring, they won every game they played for the next four years.

Sports quickly became an integral part of the new school. Student athletes compiled respectable records in many sports and even created a few dynasties. In track and field during the 1950s and 1960s, the men's team earned 11 straight conference titles. Between 1961 and 1970, Macalester's men's swimming team was nearly unbeatable, earning three national team titles at the NAIA national meet. Macalester was a leader in other areas, too: in 1971, the college hired Don Hudson to helm the football team and became the first predominantly white college to hire a black head football coach.

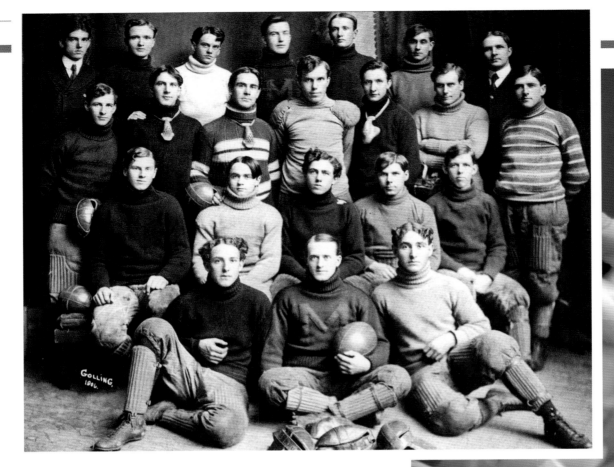

Like any college, Macalester's athletic teams also have had their struggles. Between 1974 and 1980, the school's football team had the dubious distinction of losing 50 straight contests, which some liked to term victories on moral grounds. Today's gridders certainly remember their past—they even have a motto printed on their training programs: "No more moral victories!"

Over the last two decades, Macalester has become known for its formidable soccer teams. Under the guidance of Coach John Leaney, Macalester's men's and women's soccer teams have become conference and national powerhouses. In 1998, the women's soccer team won the Division III NCAA tournament. The women have made 14 appearances at the national tournament and the men have appeared nine times.

Today, a new athletic and wellness complex and coaches with national reputations are building Macalester's athletic strength and proving that excellence can be achieved both in the classroom and on the athletic field.

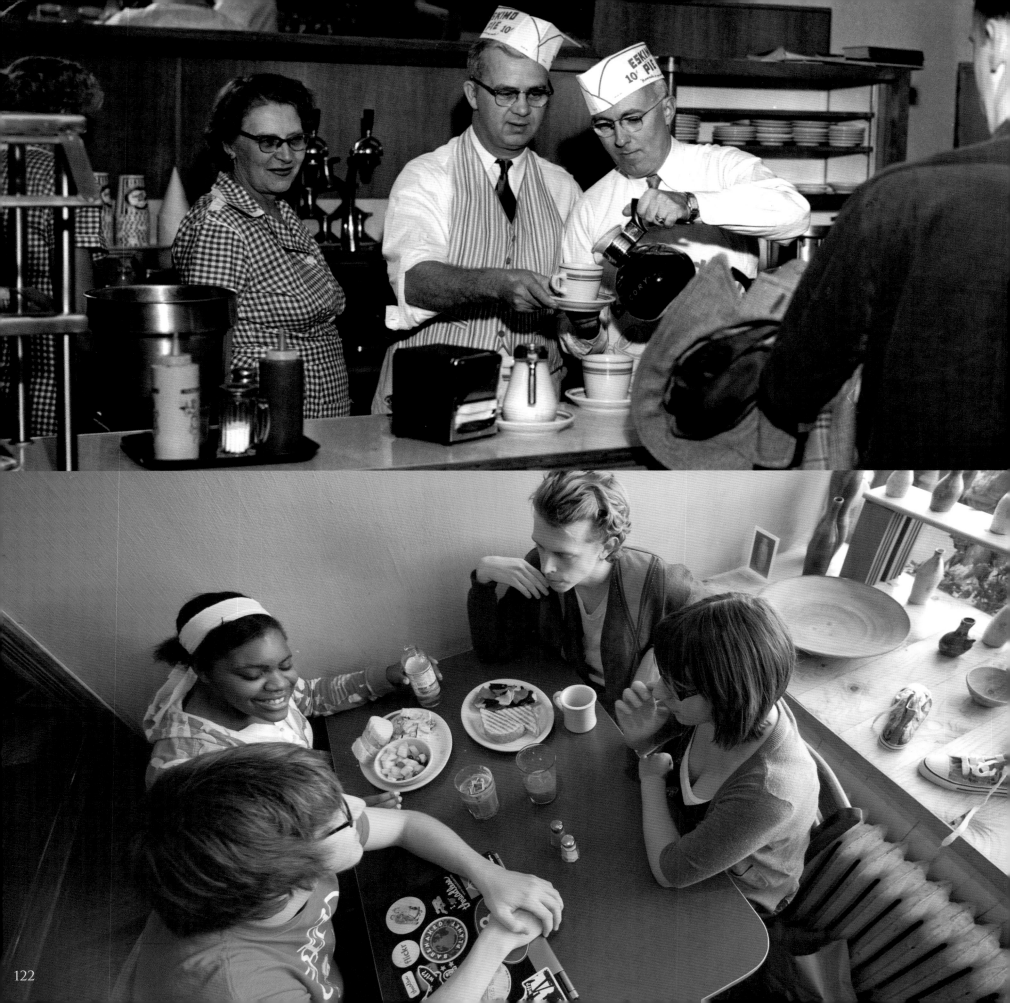

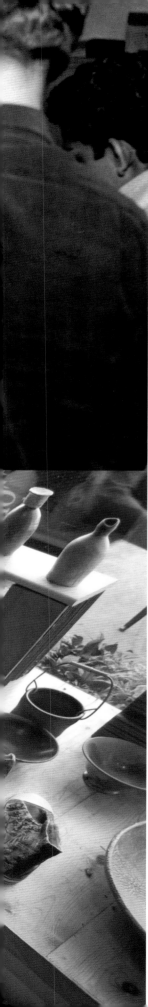

IN THE NEIGHBORHOOD

The backdrop of the campus, Grand Avenue and the surrounding residential neighborhood, has always been a key part of the Macalester experience. Through good times and bad, Macalester has made an active effort to preserve the beauty and health of the area.

During Macalester's early years, Grand Avenue was lined with magnificent homes, but during the 1930s and 1940s, many began to deteriorate. Some were turned into apartments and allowed to fall into disrepair.

By the 1960s and 1970s, a new generation of homeowners interested in historic preservation began to buy the houses and restore them. At the same time, however, urban unrest threatened to drive business owners out of the central city.

Thanks in part to work done by geography professor David Lanegran '63 and his students, Grand Avenue merchants and residents along with city officials developed a plan to build on the area's history and create a thriving neighborhood.

Eschewing chain restaurants and strip malls, neighborhood associations encouraged pedestrian-friendly streets and sidewalks, independent stores, and building restoration. As hoped, the changes convinced residents to stay in the neighborhood for their purchases rather than heading downtown or to the suburbs. Coffee shops, like the original Dunn Bros that opened near the college in 1987, encouraged students and neighbors to gather and engage in conversation. The Hungry Mind Bookstore (and later, Ruminator Books) was a longtime neighborhood favorite, bringing in countless national authors for readings from 1970 until its closing in 2004. Grand Avenue became not only a strong neighborhood asset but a highly successful regional destination for shopping and dining.

Macalester has continued its concerted effort to be a good neighbor. Its High Winds Fund, established by DeWitt Wallace in 1956, manages several houses and commercial buildings near campus. Staff members reach out to nearby residents to ensure that neighbors are aware and supportive of Macalester work that might affect the neighborhood. They've also formed partnerships with vital neighborhood organizations including the Neighborhood Energy Connection and Family Tree Clinic. Staff members help lead neighborhood partnerships that seek to maintain and improve the neighborhood for the benefit of students, faculty, staff, and neighbors.

AS HOPED,
THE CHANGES
CONVINCED
RESIDENTS TO
STAY IN THE
NEIGHBORHOOD
FOR THEIR
PURCHASES
RATHER THAN
HEADING
DOWNTOWN
OR TO THE
SUBURBS.

LASSIES CARRY MAC ANNIVERSARY CAKE

Each member of the Mac clan attending Founder's Day celebration last Saturday received a piece of this birthday cake absolutely free.
Shown above keeping a not-too-Scotch guard on the bonnie pastry, which seems, in altitude, to rival the heathered highlands, are, left to right,
Jean Anderson, Ardie Hillman, Barbara Lee Durkee and Eleanor Siegler. —The Mac Weekly

FOUNDERS DAY

Macites celebrated the first Founders Day in March 1938. The bash celebrated the 1874 chartering of the school and included many "plaid effects," according to the event's planning committee. The college held regular Founders Day events until they were abandoned in the 1970s due to a lack of student interest.

In 2004, Macalester held a semi-formal Inaugural Gala celebrating both the inauguration of President Brian C. Rosenberg and the college's 130th birthday (a huge birthday cake was part of the festivities). Students enjoyed the event so much it was brought back as Founders Day and has been an annual event ever since.

ALUMNI REUNION

Each year in early summer, more than 1,000 alumni and families gather on campus for a weekend of fun, food, memories, music, faculty talks, and other activites that celebrate the lasting Macalester connection.

the Continuity *of* Macalester

When Edward Duffield Neill founded Macalester, he intended for the school to educate students who would take action and serve others. He intended for Macalester students to make positive differences in their own neighborhoods and around the world, just as he had.

Creating a college to prepare such students was not easy. Sustaining such a college was equally difficult; financial hardships threatened on many occasions to erode quality and even to put the college out of business.

Throughout its history, Macalester has been guided by strong leaders who preserved its founder's values even in the most difficult times. Meanwhile, generous stewards have helped Macalester build on its strengths, consistently improve upon its already high standards, and offer meaningful new opportunities to students of each generation. While the late DeWitt Wallace single-handedly helped Macalester reach new levels of institutional strength on more than one occasion, the 21st century has seen unprecedented numbers of alumni joining together to broaden the college's base of support for the future.

The story of Macalester College, its strengths and successes, and the lives of its alumni, is a story that is still being lived.

1874

A TIMELINE OF NOTABLE PEOPLE

1874   On March 5, the State of Minnesota formally charters Macalester College. The college's founder, Reverend Edward Duffield Neill, has already worked for 20 years to establish a private college in Minnesota; a significant gift from prominent Philadelphia businessman and philanthropist Charles Macalester finally makes this possible. As the college's first president, Neill spends another 10 years seeking operating support to hire faculty and enroll students. (See Neill's biography, page 142.)

1884   Reverend Thomas A. McCurdy becomes Macalester's second president after trustees promise to raise an additional $100,000, hire a fiscal secretary, and release McCurdy from fundraising duties after six months. McCurdy promises free tuition to ministerial candidates at the all-male school, and pays professors the handsome sum of $2,000 a year. However, the school's fiscal challenges make McCurdy an unpopular president, and he returns to the ministry in 1890.

1885   In September, Macalester opens with five professors, six first-year college students, and 52 preparatory students.

Above: *Founding benefactor Charles Macalester.*
L to R: *Professor and President James Wallace (back row left) with faculty baseball team, Professor G. Theodore Mitau, Dean Margaret Doty, the Class of 1891, President Charles Turck in uniform during World War II, Yahya Armajani*

1885   1890   1907   1924

1890   Reverend David James Burrell spends just over a year as president of Macalester, splitting his duties as the head of the college with his responsibilities as minister of Minneapolis's Westminster Presbyterian Church.

1892   Reverend Adam Weir Ringland begins a two-year stint as Macalester's fourth president, during which he persuades the trustees to open the college to women.

1894   James Wallace, a respected professor of classical studies since 1887, agrees to serve as Macalester's fifth president. During his 12-year presidency, he raises money to pay off Macalester's debts, increases the size of the student body, and helps establish a million-dollar endowment; then he returns to the faculty. Throughout his career, he sets the highest of academic standards for the young college. (See Wallace's biography, page 144.)

1907   Thomas Morey Hodgman begins his 10-year presidency; under his leadership the college builds a dorm for women and Carnegie Science Hall.

1918   Reverend Elmer Allen Bess serves as Macalester's president for six years, presiding over a successful campaign that raises nearly a million dollars.

1924   John Carey Acheson begins his term as the eighth president of Macalester. A prodigious fundraiser, Acheson helps prevent Macalester from going bankrupt during the Great Depression. Particularly valuable is the relationship Acheson has developed with DeWitt Wallace, son of former president James Wallace and a major benefactor of the college.

1924   Margaret Doty '14 joins Macalester as dean of women, a post she holds for more than 35 years. She becomes known for her ability to remember all students' names and for her campaign to allow dancing at the college, a rule that was not formalized until 1930.

1940   1943   1957

1940   Ted Mitau, a young Jewish man who fled Nazi Germany in 1937, graduates from Macalester. He goes on to teach at the school for decades, becoming one of the college's most demanding and respected professors.

1943   Hubert H. Humphrey arrives at Macalester to teach political science for a year. After an unsuccessful presidential bid in 1968, he returns to teach from 1969 to 1971.

1946   Renowned historian Yahya Armajani, a native of Iran, begins his 28-year teaching career at Macalester. (See Armajani's biography, page 141.)

1946   Walter Mondale enrolls at the college. With Hubert Humphrey as a mentor, Mondale goes on to become a U.S. senator, vice president, and ambassador to Japan.

1957   Ruth DeBeer graduates. She becomes a noted authority on fitness and wellness as well as a trustee and generous supporter of the college. The Ruth Stricker Dayton Campus Center is named in her honor.

L to R: *President Charles Turck with Hubert Humphrey and a young Walter Mondale '50 circa 1947, Ruth DeBeer (now Ruth Stricker Dayton) and fellow Bigelow Hall resident, President James Robinson, President Harvey Rice with Fannie Mac*

1961 *1968* *1971*

1958   Harvey Mitchell Rice, former president of New York State University's Buffalo and Oswego campuses, becomes Macalester's tenth president. During his tenure, he oversees the $32 million "Macalester Challenge Campaign" that transforms the college. More than a dozen buildings are built or renovated during his tenure, the size of the faculty doubles, and the college's reputation and recruitment spread nationally.

1961   Kofi Annan graduates. He begins a career with the United Nations shortly after graduating, later becoming secretary-general of the organization. He receives the Nobel Peace Prize for his U.N. work in 2001.

1968   Arthur S. Flemming, U. S. Secretary of Health, Education, and Welfare under President Eisenhower and former president of Ohio Wesleyan University and the University of Oregon, begins his three-year tenure with the college. He oversees creation of the Expanded Educational Opportunities (EEO) program, which brings a greater range of social, economic, racial, and cultural diversity to the college. After leaving Macalester, he serves on the U.S. Commission on Civil Rights.

1971   James A. Robinson, previously vice president and provost at Ohio State, becomes Macalester's 12th president. He is the youngest person to hold the position when he takes the helm at age 39. Budgetary troubles force Robinson to spend much of his time fundraising.

1975   1984   2003

1975   As the college's 13th president, John B. Davis Jr. leads the college back to financial self-sufficiency and re-establishes a good relationship with college benefactor DeWitt Wallace, who had withdrawn support during Macalester's financial difficulties.

1984   Robert M. Gavin Jr. takes the helm as Macalester's president. During his presidency, he leads a strong effort to increase academic rigor, improves the college's academic reputation, recruits students worldwide, and oversees the renovation of many campus buildings.

1996   Michael S. McPherson becomes the institution's 15th president. A nationally known economist, McPherson raises $55 million through the Touch the Future campaign. The funding helps support academic programs, financial aid, student-faculty research opportunities, and the construction of the Ruth Stricker Dayton Campus Center.

2003   Dickens scholar Brian C. Rosenberg joins Macalester as its 16th president. Among highlights of his tenure are the development of the Institute for Global Citizenship and the Leonard Center, a new athletic and recreation center.

PROFILES IN EXCELLENCE

CATHARINE DEAVER LEALTAD '15

Catharine Lealtad '15 may be best known by the Macalester community as the first African American to graduate from the college, but she made her mark in the world for her talent as a physician, her tireless advocacy for human rights, and her commitment to helping underserved populations around the world. Even in retirement, she spent many of her days working at free clinics and writing letters to politicians.

Lealtad, a St. Paul native, was among Macalester's most gifted students when she enrolled in 1911. She graduated four years later with high honors in both of her majors, chemistry and history. She was particularly moved by President James Wallace, who impressed upon her the obligation to help others. After stints at the YWCA and Urban League in New York, she earned a medical degree in Europe.

Her work carried her from Chicago to Harlem, and during World War II she went to Germany to supervise medical services for displaced children. She was transferred from Germany to China in 1946, where she spent two years on a mission to fight cholera, more than half of which was behind enemy lines. Later, she worked in the pediatrics unit of New York's Sydenham Hospital, the first voluntary interracial hospital.

Her retirement in 1968 did little to slow her down: "When you are alert and alive, doing nothing is extremely boring." She went to Mexico City, where she worked full days in a free clinic until fainting spells forced her to return home.

Lealtad is the only person to have received two honorary degrees from Macalester, one for her career and a second for her work following "retirement." She died in 1989, but her legacy continues: In 1993, she was recognized in *African American Women: A Biographical Dictionary* alongside luminaries including Rosa Parks, Toni Morrison, and Gwendolyn Brooks. In 2002, the college's new center for multicultural life was named the Lealtad-Suzuki Center.

SHE WAS RECOGNIZED IN *AFRICAN AMERICAN WOMEN: A BIOGRAPHICAL DICTIONARY* ALONGSIDE LUMINARIES INCLUDING ROSA PARKS, TONI MORRISON, AND GWENDOLYN BROOKS.

ESTHER TORII SUZUKI '46

Just two hours before she was scheduled to go to a Japanese American internment camp in September 1942, 16-year-old Esther Torii received a telegram from the U.S. government: she had been released so she could attend Macalester College. She would be the first Japanese American student to graduate from the school.

The last-minute telegram was both exciting and terrifying. She had spent long months finding funding, getting a letter of acceptance from President Charles Turck, and securing letters of recommendation from others attesting to her loyalty, but the note meant she'd have to leave her family. She quickly repacked her belongings in her family's only suitcase and boarded a train to Minnesota.

Though the transition wasn't easy—she recalled being yelled at by train conductors and breaking down in tears when she received a letter reporting that members of her family were ill—she also acknowledged the kindness shown to her by students, professors, parents, and administrators. They offered her weekly dinners, good advice, and places to stay during school holidays. She kept in touch with many long after she graduated.

After receiving her degree in sociology, Suzuki became a social worker in the St. Paul area. She was active in civil rights groups and developed programs to help other Asians and Asian Americans whose lives were disrupted by war. She also maintained close ties with Macalester, spending six years on the college's Alumni Board and receiving an Alumni Service Award for her efforts. She died in 1999 at age 73. In 2002, the Lealtad-Suzuki Center was created to provide multicultural training, development, and programming for the Macalester community.

THE FIRST JAPANESE AMERICAN STUDENT
TO GRADUATE FROM THE SCHOOL.

YAHYA ARMAJANI

When historian Yahya Armajani arrived on Macalester's campus in 1946, he expected to stay just long enough to speak as part of a lecture tour. Thanks to President Charles Turck, who recognized his talent immediately and offered him a position on the faculty, Armajani spent nearly three decades at the school. His students remember him not only because he pushed them to expand their intellectual horizons, but because of his warmth and humor.

Armajani was born in Siahkal, Iran, in 1908. His parents did not read or write, but he excelled in school. He eventually earned a PhD from Princeton and was ordained a Presbyterian minister.

While he spent his adult life in the United States, he remained devoted to Iran and was a national authority on Middle East history. He worked

tirelessly to promote international understanding by publishing books, giving lectures, and broadening perspectives one student at a time. His teaching earned both local and national awards.

Armajani spoke out frequently about civil rights for all Americans, and in a letter to the Macalester campus announcing his retirement, he noted that Macalester's "future greatness" depended on students willing to stand up for their convictions. His letter came not long after student protests linked to a range of funding cuts. "Those who do not respond to challenges die in bed without bruises, but those who respond make mistakes," he wrote. "It is not the mistakes, however, which abide but the positive results of the response, and there are many."

Each year, a Macalester international student who embodies the values espoused by Armajani receives a prize named for him.

HIS STUDENTS REMEMBER HIM NOT ONLY BECAUSE HE PUSHED THEM TO EXPAND THEIR INTELLECTUAL HORIZONS, BUT BECAUSE OF HIS WARMTH AND HUMOR.

LEADING THE WAY

EDWARD DUFFIELD NEILL

When Macalester College officially came into being in 1874, it was the result of the sheer tenacity of founder Edward Duffield Neill.

Neill had spent decades trying to get a Christian men's college off the ground, thwarted by funding trouble, untimely deaths, and even war. Over time, the modest buildings that once sprouted on the windswept prairie have been transformed into a beautiful and bustling urban campus. Meanwhile, the values Neill hoped to instill have remained remarkably constant: the pursuit of academic excellence, a commitment to service, and a willingness to explore the wider world with compassion and thoughtfulness.

Neill arrived in Minnesota in 1848, a Presbyterian missionary preacher whose greatest passion was education. His work as superintendent for public instruction for the territory from 1851 to 1853 and later as chancellor of the University of Minnesota helped establish the entire Minnesota school system.

His personal goal, though, was to start an institution of higher learning similar to Amherst, his alma mater. A bright and engaging young man—he entered college at age 14—he was adept at building enthusiasm for his ideas.

During an 1851 trip to meet with church leaders in Philadelphia, he convinced locomotive builder William Baldwin to donate $1,500 to start a private academy in St. Paul. Construction of the Baldwin school started immediately, and he first class enrolled in 1853.

When Neill broadened his plans to include a Christian men's college, he again contacted Baldwin to help fund the project. Neill told him in a letter that he hoped the school would not only provide a solid education, but would keep men from spending too much time at the local "saloons and gambling establishments." Baldwin liked Neill's plan and provided $5,000 for the venture.

In 1855, Neill's second school, the College of St. Paul, opened with 34 students. However, the school was destined to fail. An economic depression, the development of a free public school system, and rumors of war hobbled the Baldwin School and the College of St. Paul—education seemed like a luxury, not a necessity.

In 1861, with the schools already in dire straights, Neill left his post to become chaplain of the First Minnesota Regiment in the Civil War. Without his guidance, both schools closed.

During his time away, he began attracting national attention. He was appointed a secretary to Abraham Lincoln in 1864, and in 1869 President Andrew Johnson nominated him for the post of Commissioner of Education. Other commitments, however, did not allow him to accept the position.

Neill returned to Minnesota in 1872, where he used his own money to start a new college, Jesus College, in a vacant hotel known as Winslow House. Abysmal marketing kept him from attracting students or funding, and he soon abandoned his plans.

However, he still saw opportunity with the vacant hotel. Winslow House was owned by a wealthy Philadelphian, Charles Macalester, and he sent earnest letters to Macalester pleading for his help. Initially resistant, Macalester eventually agreed to deed the house to Neill to develop the college, so long as the school was named after him.

On March 5, 1874, the State of Minnesota officially chartered Macalester College. It would be 11 years before college-level classes were held (though preparatory classes were available), and by the time the first college class enrolled in 1885, the original building had been sold, and the institution was relocated to its current site.

Neill's persistence won out in the end, and University of Minnesota founder William Folwell Watts said Neill had a deserved reputation as "Minnesota's apostle of education."

MEANWHILE, THE VALUES NEILL HOPED TO INSTILL HAVE REMAINED REMARKABLY CONSTANT: THE PURSUIT OF ACADEMIC EXCELLENCE, A COMMITMENT TO SERVICE, AND A WILLINGNESS TO EXPLORE THE WIDER WORLD WITH COMPASSION AND THOUGHTFULNESS.

JAMES WALLACE

With the exception of founder Edward Duffield Neill, no man had as much impact on the early success and character of Macalester as James Wallace. He played an active role at Macalester for five decades, serving as a professor in its earliest days, as president for more than a decade, and, for at least one year, right fielder on the faculty baseball team.

Wallace arrived at Macalester in 1887 with a sterling reputation as a professor of Greek and modern languages. He was a popular, engaging teacher, and he remained devoted to the school even in its darkest days. When financial instability kept the college from paying salaries to faculty members, Wallace sent his family back to Ohio to live with his in-laws and he spent his winter evenings sitting on a radiator and wearing a coat to keep warm.

His remarkable loyalty and strong character made him a good choice to lead the institution at a time of crisis. Two presidents left the school after very short terms, unable to raise enough funds to keep the college going. Wallace took the helm in 1894 and stayed on for a dozen years, helping to stabilize the young and growing institution.

As president, Wallace had to contend with one fiscal crisis after another, but through great persistence and personal sacrifice, he was able to raise the funds to pay off the college's debt and even to build a small endowment. Over several years, he built solid relationships with philanthropists such as George Draper Dayton, Frederick Weyerhaeuser, and James J. Hill. He also convinced steel magnate Andrew Carnegie to provide funding for a much-needed science building just before he left office. After taking a sabbatical in New York, he returned to teach for many more years.

Though Wallace rarely had an easy year while at Macalester, he displayed a good sense of humor. He is perhaps best known today for his dry response to a college practical joke. When Wallace arrived on the third floor of Old Main to lecture, he found a cow had been led up the stairs by student pranksters (which included, the story goes, his son DeWitt). He took one look at the cow and said in a deadpan voice, "Whoever brought the cow up will please remove it."

Wallace loved the outdoors and played sports for many years. Records indicate he played on the faculty baseball team until he was at least 62. He may not have been the most talented member of the team, but he was probably the most stylish: he is the only one sporting a fedora in the team photo.

Wallace's work, up until his death in 1939 at the age of 90, made an indelible mark on the college. If the sacrifices were considerable, seeing Macalester grow and develop made them worthwhile. "It [was] the joy of my life," he said.

CHARLES TURCK

When Charles Turck became president of Macalester in 1939, the college had been in a period of stagnation: enrollment had slowed, buildings needed improvements, and the endowment required serious attention. During his two decades as president, he used his considerable skills to improve the faculty, add to the campus, stabilize college finances, and provide a deep sense of commitment to internationalism and service. Much of his work—from campus buildings to his philosophy about the role of the college—remains today.

Turck's first connection with the college came several years before he assumed the presidency, when he had a luncheon with several Macalester faculty members, including James Wallace. "I was tremendously impressed with Dr. Wallace," he later recalled. "He was a magnificent speaker, a courageous man, and an outright internationalist in the midst of an isolationist state. He hit me just right." When Turck was offered the presidency at Macalester a few years later, that conversation with Wallace played a role in his decision to accept the job. "Here was a chance to advance the cause of the international spirit, without which our world is doomed," he said. His conversation with Wallace convinced him that his beliefs would be well received at Macalester.

Turck had a knack for spotting talent: he hired several faculty members whose stellar teaching and long careers made them legends, including Ted Mitau and Hildegard Binder Johnson. When Yahya Armajani came to give a campus talk, Turck promptly offered him a job. These three hires—Jewish, female, Iranian—set a new precedent for inclusiveness. His insistence that faculty members be free to pursue their interests and express their views, no

matter how controversial, added an edginess to the college's character. So did his own very prominent advocacy of issues of his day—U.S. entry into World War II as a means to world justice, and later the absolute necessity for racial and economic justice at home. "We are living now in a world that must be a world of brotherhood or it will cease to be," he said. In 1950, he raised the U.N. flag on campus, just a few years after the organization was founded. It has flown every day since then.

Turck's desire to get students to see and understand the wider world was ahead of its time. Under his guidance, Macalester launched a study abroad program and introduced a major in international relations. He used a weekly column in the student newspaper to address problems faced daily in America, including human rights. "We must be careful that no word or act of ours supports or encourages . . . prejudicial attitude[s] or action[s]," he wrote in reference to an athletic boycott in Louisiana and Georgia, where integration was not allowed on the basketball court.

His earnest beliefs in internationalism, faculty freedom, and abolishing prejudice were tempered by a lively wit. When Margaret Doty, the dean of women, complained to Turck that she could see men and women lying next to one another on the campus lawn one warm spring day, he gave her his best advice: "I'd pull down the shade and pray for rain," he said.

During his tenure, which included World War II and the Korean War, Turck shifted the curriculum to include far more vocational and professional training courses. During the war, students could take classes on Morse Code and map reading; they could also enroll in nursing, business administration, and other programs. Eventually, the college returned to its emphasis on a classic liberal arts education.

The student body grew quickly during Turck's years, and so did the physical plant—student dorms, a health center, a student union, and a library were added. By the time he resigned in 1958, the student population had nearly doubled. Thanks to a relationship he nurtured with DeWitt Wallace, Turck was also able to add considerably to the endowment by the time he left his post.

TOWARD A SECURE FINANCIAL FOUNDATION

Money—and lack of it—has played a recurring role in Macalester's history. Philanthropist Charles Macalester provided the gift that established the college, but founder Edward Duffield Neill spent 11 more years raising funds to get the college open in September 1885. In truth, he lacked the continuing donors that keep a private college running, and during its first 15 years of operation, Macalester was in constant financial crisis: creditors threatened to foreclose, faculty salaries went unpaid in order to pay other debt, and the young college nearly closed on several occasions.

By about 1900, heroic fundraising efforts by President James Wallace had retired the college's debt. A small but devoted group of supporters contributed regularly to operations, and eventually notable businessmen—including George Draper Dayton, Frederick Weyerhaeuser, James J. Hill, Andrew Carnegie, Cyrus McCormick, and John Converse—established a million-dollar endowment in hopes of providing financial stability for the future.

The Great Depression put an end to that stability. Faculty members took 30 percent salary cuts, and when the college tried to increase tuition, enrollment dropped precipitously. During the 1930s, however, President John Acheson developed a relationship with DeWitt Wallace, son of retired president and professor James Wallace. A former Macalester student, DeWitt had founded the wildly successful *Reader's Digest* and was willing to give generously to his alma mater. Over the next several decades he and his wife, Lila Acheson Wallace, gave more than $50 million for buildings, scholarships, and programs. A $10 million challenge gift for the college's $32 million campaign in the 1960s helped reshape the campus and was among the largest gifts to a college anywhere at the time.

Even this gift could not ensure stability. The economic recession of the late 1960s and early 1970s, combined with six years of sharply curtailed giving by Wallace, forced Macalester to cut programs and eliminate faculty and staff positions. Though Macalester was not without company—some 22 small colleges closed their doors in 1970 alone—the pain was substantial.

At left, Janet Wallace Fine Arts Center.
At right, Lila Acheson Wallace and DeWitt Wallace '11, the stadium

In 1976, President John B. Davis Jr. succeeded in rebuilding Macalester's relationship with Wallace, who once again provided support including a significant bequest of stock in the *Reader's Digest* Association. When RDA went public in the early 1990s, Wallace's final gift leapt in value and helped lift the college's relatively small endowment to a new level. Income generated by the endowment enabled Macalester to make significant improvements in its faculty size, facilities, recruitment efforts, and programs, including those involving the college's distinctive international and cultural diversity as well as civic engagement efforts.

Because of complex financial requirements the endowment could not be fully diversified until 2002, and it did not participate in the huge market gains of the 1990s. Since 2002, however, the endowment has enjoyed better-than-average earnings and has been diversified into a portfolio designed to withstand the extremes of the market. By policy, spending is limited, with the goal of benefiting not only current students, but every generation yet to come. And while the endowment was created by captains of industry and given a significant boost by a canny magazine entrepreneur, modern gift-planning measures mean that new endowed funds are established by teachers, doctors, and clergy along with financial analysts, software developers, and executives.

Meanwhile, the 21st century has brought sharply increased individual support, especially by alumni. Among the beneficial effects: the college sustains its commitment to economic diversity by providing unusually high levels of financial aid. In 2007–08, for example, 65 percent of first-year students received aid averaging $25,600 per student. Another positive trend: the college has operated with a balanced budget every year since 1975. Quite a change from 100 years earlier.

SECOND CENTURY

Exceptional leadership, including that of the college's most recent presidents, has helped make Macalester among the most respected colleges in the nation.

Restoring Confidence

When John B. Davis Jr. assumed the top spot at Macalester in 1975, the college was foundering. The institution was struggling financially, and lax spending policies had alienated its major donor, DeWitt Wallace.

Davis steered Macalester back on track. He reigned in spending and pledged to balance the budget. Equally important, he helped to restore morale among faculty and staff, which had slipped as Macalester slid into financial difficulties. Davis also charted a course that significantly boosted the academic credentials of incoming students and faculty.

This ambitious plan helped him regain the trust of Wallace, whose support became legendary. With the help of Wallace's generous gifts, the college was able to add major scholarship programs and build a stronger endowment. It also improved many of its facilities and computing capabilities as a result of the increased support of Wallace and others.

From Stability to Strength

When Robert M. Gavin became president in 1984, the college held a much stronger financial position. Gavin was committed to maintaining that financial strength while elevating Macalester's academic profile.

At the time, Macalester was a well-respected regional college, but Gavin set out to make it competitive with the best schools in the nation. On his watch, the college hired additional faculty while holding student enrollment steady. With a lower student-faculty ratio, students had more opportunities to collaborate with faculty on research and writing projects.

Gavin pushed to hire faculty with exceptional credentials, and he challenged them to achieve more to earn tenure. He also supported efforts to attract top students from around the nation.

As he worked to improve the academic profile of the college, he also emphasized the importance of internationalism, a goal first articulated by Charles Turck. The college began enrolling a greater number of international students, and it added programs to allow more students to study abroad.

By the time Gavin resigned in 1996, Macalester had become one of the most respected academic institutions in the nation. More important, it had done so while retaining its long-held values of internationalism, service, and a diverse campus population.

Continuing Excellence

Michael McPherson arrived at Macalester in 1996, a time of unprecedented strength for the college. McPherson, an economist, was committed to securing the longterm future of the college through strategic planning and fundraising.

He embarked on the college's most ambitious comprehensive campaign, called Touch the Future, which raised more than $55 million. During his tenure, the college diversified and stabilized its endowment, which had been almost entirely dependent on the health of Reader's Digest stock.

McPherson oversaw significant changes to the campus community—and the campus itself. The college created new positions to support multicultural initiatives and increased support to encourage civic engagement. The Ruth Stricker Dayton Campus Center and a new residence hall were completed as well.

When McPherson left to head up the Spencer Foundation, Macalester had increased its national visibility and, with a newly diversified and solidly managed endowment, was on its way to more solid financial footing.

A Vision for the Future

Since arriving at Macalester in 2003, Brian C. Rosenberg has consistently emphasized the importance of educating global citizens willing and able to serve their communities and of alumni acting as responsible stewards of the college.

He created the Institute for Global Citizenship, including a new sustainably designed and constructed building to house its programs and faculty. He also led the planning and construction of the new Leonard Center, which houses recreation, health, and wellness facilities as well as social and event space to help foster a stronger community. Together wtih many faculty and staff, he has worked to deepen Macalester's connections to the urban life og the Twin Cities.

In 2008, the college began the public phase of its Step Forward campaign, a comprehensive $150 million effort to increase funds for financial aid, create more international opportunities for students and faculty, support capital projects, and increase Annual Fund support.

The presidents of the past 30 years have built on the work of their predecessors as well as that of students, alumni, parents, faculty, and staff to sustain the college's values, make its programs nationally known, provide more opportunities to more students, and create graduates who are well prepared for an increasingly global society.

A REPUTATION FOR EXCELLENCE AND ACTION

When Macalester's second president, Thomas McCurdy, stepped to the front of the college chapel to address students and visitors in the fall of 1885, he was happy to share his optimism for the future of the institution. "[The] prospects of the college," he said to a packed house, "are wonderful."

The character and accomplishments of its graduates speak volumes about the character of the college. And as ever-greater media attention is focused on how colleges compare with one another, Macalester bubbles to the top again and again. Its high academic standards are frequently lauded by publications including *Newsweek* and *U.S. News and World Report*, and student guides praise the school as "the ultimate preparation for success in academia, law, medicine, social service, and business" and as an institution that combines "academic rigor with global perspective."

David Bell '65, former CEO of Interpublic Group and Bozell Worldwide, helps crystallize the noteworthy values of Macalester: "As I look back at the gifts Macalester gave me," he says, "I think about global consciousness, leadership opportunities and experience, and an understanding of the need for giving back through service. It is in the Mac DNA."

President McCurdy's speech may be more than 120 years old, but its message is as relevant as ever. Today, says President Rosenberg, "Our success is best measured by the books our graduates choose to read, the philanthropic causes for which they labor, the things they build and re-build, the positions of leadership they occupy, the children they raise—in short, by the lives they lead."

Presidents *and* Trustees

Presidents of Macalester College

The Rev. Edward Duffield Neill,* D.D.	1874–1884
The Rev. Thomas A. McCurdy,* D.D.	1884–1890
The Rev. David James Burrell,* D.D.	1890–1891
The Rev. Adam Weir Ringland,* D.D.	1892–1894
James Wallace,* Ph.D., LL.D., D.D.	1894–1906
Thomas Morey Hodgman,* LL.D.	1907–1917
The Rev. Elmer Allen Bess,* D.D.	1918–1923
John Carey Acheson,* A.M., LL.D.	1924–1937
Charles Joseph Turck,* A.M., LL.B., LL.D.	1939–1958
Harvey Mitchell Rice,* A.M., Ph.D., L.H.D., LL.D.	1958–1968
Arthur S. Flemming,* A.B., M.A., J.D.	1968–1971
James A. Robinson, A.A., A.B., M.A., Ph.D.	1971–1975
John B. Davis, Jr., B.A., M.Ed., E.Ed., LL.D.	1975–1984
Robert M. Gavin, Jr., B.A., Ph.D.	1984–1996
Michael S. McPherson, B.A., M.A., Ph.D.	1996–2003
Brian C. Rosenberg, B.A., M.A., Ph.D.	2003–

*Deceased

Chairs of the Macalester College Board of Trustees

Charles E. Vanderburgh	1885–1886
Joseph C. Whitney	1886–1893
John B. Donaldson	1893–1897
Thomas H. Dickson	1897–1901
Thomas Shaw	1901–1918
Angus McLeod	1918–1921
George D. Dayton	1921–1925
Charles H. Bigelow	1925–1936
Frederic R. Bigelow	1937–1946
David J. Winton	1947–1949
Arnold H. Lowe	1949–1959
Frederick L. Deming	1959–1963
George D. Dayton, II	1963–1967
Archibald B. Jackson	1967–1971
W. John Driscoll	1971–1974
Donald E. Garretson P '74	1974–1977
Carl B. Drake	1977–1979
Richard L. Schall '51	1979–1982
F. T. Weyerhaeuser	1982–1985
David A. Ranheim '64	1985–1989
Mary Lee Dayton GP '06	1989–1992
Barbara Armajani '63	1992–1994
Timothy A. Hultquist '72	1995–2000
Mark A. Vander Ploeg '74	2000–2006
Jeffrey B. Larson '79, P '10	2006–2007
Timothy D. Hart-Andersen P '12	2007–2008
David Deno '79, P '11	2008–

The Board of Trustees of Macalester College   2008–2009

DEAR OLD MACALESTER EVER THE SAME, TO THOSE WHOSE

THY SONS, LOVED BY ALL THY DAUGHTERS. HAIL HAIL TO

CHAMPIONS, FOR THEE WE'LL FIGHT AND PRAY, ALL THY N

HAIL, HAIL TO THEE, OUR COLLEGE DEAR THY NAME SHA

THINE HONOR FAR EVER OUR HEARTS TO THEE CLING W

ARTS ARE THRILLED BY THY DEAR NAME. CHERISHED BY ALL

EE OUR COLLEGE DEAR. WE ARE IN WORD AND DEED THY

S. FORWARD TO PROMINENCE. MARCH FOREVER ONWARD.

EVER BE, OUR GUIDING STAR; THY CHILDREN PROCLAIM

DEEP AFFECTION. HAIL, HAIL TO THEE, MACALESTER.

MACALESTER COLLEGE

ST. PAUL, MINNESOTA